Properties of Matter

Temperature

Arthur Best

Cavendish Square

New York

Published in 2019 by Cavendish Square Publishing, LLC
243 5th Avenue, Suite 136, New York, NY 10016

Library of Congress Cataloging-in-Publication Data

Names: Best, B. J., 1976- author.
Title: Temperature / Arthur Best.
Description: First edition. | New York : Cavendish Square, 2019. | Series: Properties of matter | Audience: K to grade 3.
Identifiers: LCCN 2018023588 (print) | LCCN 2018025014 (ebook) | ISBN 9781502642851 (ebook) |
ISBN 9781502642745 (library bound) | ISBN 9781502642837 (pbk.) | ISBN 9781502642844 (6 pack)
Subjects: LCSH: Temperature--Juvenile literature. | Concepts--Juvenile literature.
Classification: LCC QC271.4 (ebook) | LCC QC271.4 .B475 2019 (print) | DDC 536/.5--dc23
LC record available at https://lccn.loc.gov/2018023588

Editorial Director: David McNamara
Copy Editor: Nathan Heidelberger
Associate Art Director: Alan Sliwinski
Designer: Megan Metté
Production Coordinator: Karol Szymczuk
Photo Research: J8 Media

The photographs in this book are used by permission and through the courtesy of: Cover Marian Weyo/Shutterstock.com; p. 5 Wolv/iStock.com; p. 7 RapidEye/E+/Getty Images; p. 9 Samere Fahim Photography/Moment/Getty Images; p. 11 Fotosearch/Getty Images; p. 13 Tetra Images/Getty Images; p. 15 John Shepherd/iStock.com; p. 17 Robert Kneschke/Shutterstock.com; p. 19 B. A. E. Inc./Alamy Stock Photo; p. 21 Renphoto/E+/Getty Images.

Printed in the United States of America

Contents

Ice cream is cold.

It has a low temperature.

7

The sun is very hot.

It has a high temperature.

9

You can find temperature.

You use a **thermometer**.

11

Matter can change.

Heat can change it.

This ice cream is melting.

It got too hot.

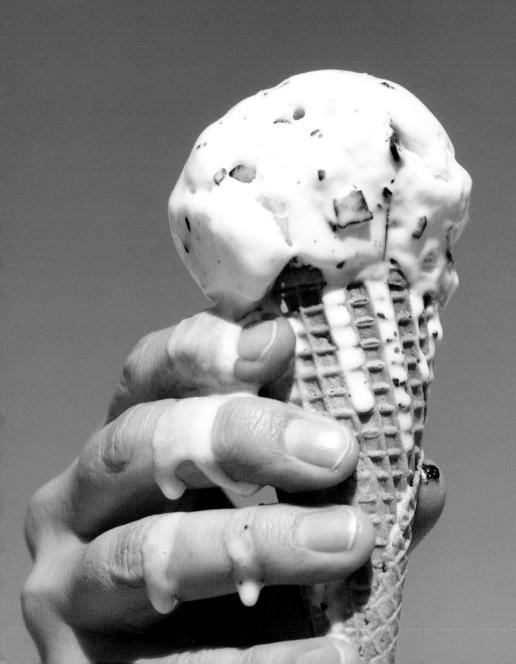

13

Matter is a solid if it is hard.

Ice is a solid.

It is hard water.

It is cold.

Water is a **liquid**.

It flows.

It is not too cold.

It is not too hot.

Water can become a **gas**.

It is hot.

Water turns into steam.

People have a temperature.

This kid is too hot.

She has a fever.

She is sick!

21

New Words

gas (GAAS) Very light matter, like air.

liquid (LIK-wid) Something that flows.

matter (MAT-er) What things are made of.

temperature (TEM-per-cher) How hot or cold something is.

thermometer (thur-MOM-ih-ter) A tool to find temperature.

Index

About the Author

Arthur Best lives in Wisconsin with his wife and son. He has written many other books for children. He likes liquid water best.

About BOOKWORMS

Bookworms help independent readers gain reading confidence through high-frequency words, simple sentences, and strong picture/text support. Each book explores a concept that helps children relate what they read to the world they live in.